WESLEY'S CHAPEL

Contents

Above:
The east end of the chapel.

Right:
A motif from the gallery frieze. It includes a dove representing the Holy Spirit. The snake may be the serpent of healing.

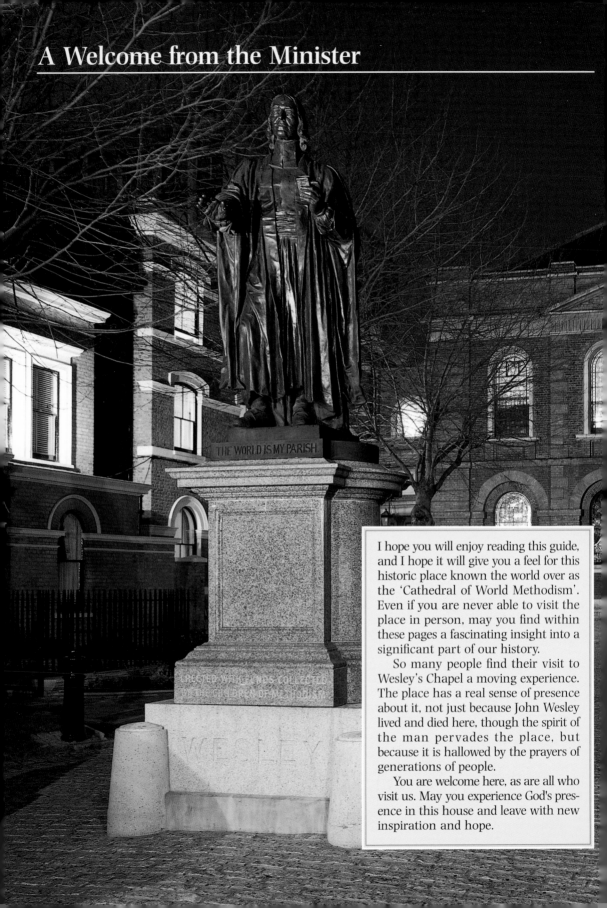

A Welcome from the Minister

THE WORLD IS MY PARISH.

ERECTED WITH FUNDS COLLECTED BY THE CHILDREN OF METHODISM.

WESLEY

I hope you will enjoy reading this guide, and I hope it will give you a feel for this historic place known the world over as the 'Cathedral of World Methodism'. Even if you are never able to visit the place in person, may you find within these pages a fascinating insight into a significant part of our history.

So many people find their visit to Wesley's Chapel a moving experience. The place has a real sense of presence about it, not just because John Wesley lived and died here, though the spirit of the man pervades the place, but because it is hallowed by the prayers of generations of people.

You are welcome here, as are all who visit us. May you experience God's presence in this house and leave with new inspiration and hope.

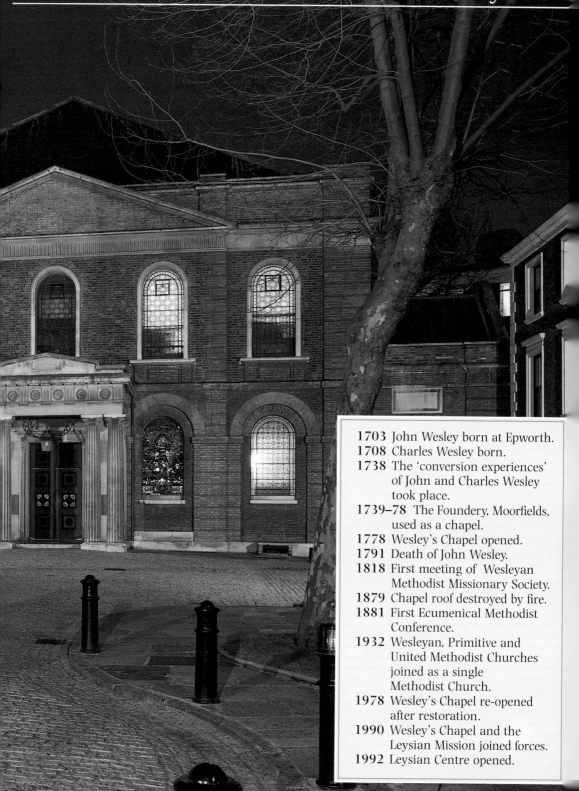

1703 John Wesley born at Epworth.
1708 Charles Wesley born.
1738 The 'conversion experiences' of John and Charles Wesley took place.
1739–78 The Foundery, Moorfields, used as a chapel.
1778 Wesley's Chapel opened.
1791 Death of John Wesley.
1818 First meeting of Wesleyan Methodist Missionary Society.
1879 Chapel roof destroyed by fire.
1881 First Ecumenical Methodist Conference.
1932 Wesleyan, Primitive and United Methodist Churches joined as a single Methodist Church.
1978 Wesley's Chapel re-opened after restoration.
1990 Wesley's Chapel and the Leysian Mission joined forces.
1992 Leysian Centre opened.

Early Years

John Wesley was born in Lincolnshire, second son of the rector of Epworth. But from his schooldays onwards his life was mostly based in London. From 1710 until 1720 he was a pupil at the Charterhouse, and for part of that time his brother Charles was at Westminster School.

The city he knew had recently risen phoenix-like from the ashes of the great fire of 1666. Foremost among the many churches rebuilt by Wren was St Paul's Cathedral. Until 1750, old London Bridge was still the only river crossing, leading to the borough of Southwark. New estates like Bloomsbury and Mayfair were developed during Wesley's lifetime; but places such as Islington, Marylebone, Chelsea and Lambeth were still villages.

During his years at Oxford, he was still within a day's ride of London. He and Charles became the centre of a group of

Above:
Charles Wesley, who played an active part in the early days of Methodism. He is now remembered mainly for his hymns.

religiously inclined students nicknamed the 'Holy Club'. Then in 1735 the two brothers set off for the new American colony of Georgia. Both were now Anglican clergymen. The venture was far from successful and on their return, each of them made once again for their circle of friends in the heart of London.

It was here, in May 1738, in the Aldersgate Street area, that first Charles Wesley and then John had experiences (often referred to as their 'conversion') which gave new life to their ministry. They were soon caught up in the Evangelical Revival in which their younger Oxford friend, George Whitefield, was already actively involved. In Bristol, John began his lifelong habit of open-air preaching, and he continued to visit Oxford. But London remained his main base.

The Wesleys were associated with the Moravian society which met in Fetter

Left: (16)
The Foundery Chapel, entered from the southern end of the vestibule, contains some of the simple wooden benches used in the old Foundery. Here too is Charles Wesley's single-manual pipe organ, which both he and his two musically gifted sons played. The hymns that Charles Wesley composed include 'Hark the herald angels sing', 'Christ the Lord is risen today' and 'Love divine, all loves excelling'.

Lane. However, growing differences over beliefs and practices led them to form a separate society in July 1740 – the first 'Methodist' society in London. It met in 'The Foundery' near Moorfields. Formerly a cannon foundry, it had been seriously damaged by an explosion in 1716 and remained unused for many years. Wesley bought the lease to the property for £115 and spent another £700 repairing and equipping it. It remained his London headquarters for almost 40 years.

The Foundery held a congregation of 1,500, with a smaller room where the classes met. In addition, it served a variety of other purposes. Here were stored the books Wesley published and sold. There was also a school for the children of the poor and the first free dispensary in London. In times of hardship, food and clothing were given out. Wesley and his preachers had their living quarters here, as did his mother in her closing years. Accommodation was provided for poor widows. Wesley insisted that all ate the same meals at the same table.

Gradually Methodist societies began to appear in towns and villages throughout the country.

Left: ⑩
A window in the north gallery commemorates the conversion of the Wesley brothers in 1738. They and two friends are seen singing Charles Wesley's 'conversion hymn' 'Where shall my wondering soul begin?' at the house of John Bray in Little Britain.

The term 'Methodist' was one of several nicknames given to members of the 'Holy Club' at Oxford, partly because of their methodical Christian life. The word became attached to John Wesley's followers after his return from Georgia, as well as to other evangelical Christians in the 18th century.

Right:
The Foundery in Wesley's day, showing the two entrances, one into the chapel, the other into the preacher's quarters and schoolroom, the small bell-turret, and Wesley's own quarters, built over the rear section of the premises. The Foundery took its name from the royal cannon foundry which formerly occupied the same premises.

The Building of the Chapel

From the early 1740s, John Wesley was travelling further and further afield, visiting Methodist societies and preaching in the fields, in market-places and wherever he could find a hearing. Neither the poor roads nor bad weather could halt him for long. But the winter months he wisely spent in London, with only short excursions into the home counties.

His other premises in London included a former Huguenot chapel in West Street near the present Cambridge Circus. Wesley insisted that Methodist preaching services should be at different times from the services in the parish church. But because West Street was a consecrated building he felt free to administer the sacrament of Holy Communion there.

By the 1770s the Methodist movement was drifting away from the Church of England. The lease of the Foundery was running out and there were plans for the residential development of Moorfields. In 1776 Wesley applied to the City of London for a new site in the area and began raising funds. The appeal was nationwide for reasons set out in his letter 'to members and friends of the Methodist societies':

'The Society at London have given assistance to their brethren in various parts of England. They have done this for upwards of thirty years; they have done it cheerfully and liberally . . . They now stand in need of assistance themselves.'

In spite of the rain a great crowd gathered for the laying of the foundation stone

Right:
Wesley's Chapel in the 1820s. The original plan was for a terrace of houses across the front of the courtyard, with access to the chapel through an archway. This was abandoned because of a decision to widen the roadway.

Below:
An imaginary reconstruction of the first Methodist Conference to be held in the new chapel in 1779. It incorporates portraits of all the preachers thought to have been present.

on 21 April 1777. In his sermon on the text 'What hath God wrought' Wesley gave a somewhat idealized account of the rise of Methodism, beginning with his Oxford days and insisting that it was no 'new religion', but simply a return to fundamentals – 'love of God and of all mankind'. He was still striving to keep the movement within the Church of England, but the building of a new chapel, to replace a multi-purpose preaching-house, was a measure of the growing respectability and independence of Methodism.

The architect was George Dance the Younger, surveyor to the City of London, who was busy laying out the nearby Finsbury estate on part of Moorfields. This accounts for the fine proportions of the Chapel and some of its more elegant features, though the overall effect was, as Wesley put it, 'perfectly neat, but not fine'.

The builder was Samuel Tooth, a class leader and local preacher belonging to the Foundery Society. Wherever Wesley travelled he was busy collecting for the building, but the work was sometimes held up by lack of funds to pay the workmen. And there were other hazards: many years later a notice was found under the floor boards

offering a reward for the recovery of workmen's tools stolen from the site.

The opening service took place on All Saints' Day, 1778. A local newspaper reported that Wesley spent the first 15 minutes of his sermon criticizing the elaborate hats worn by the women in his congregation. He had always had more sympathy for the poor and felt more at home among them, and the danger of growing affluence among his followers became an obsession in his closing years.

Below: ⑦
An 18th-century cartoon, 'The Mischief of Methodism', exhibited in the Museum of Methodism at the Chapel.

Over the years there have, inevitably, been changes, so that the present interior is a blend of old and new. When it was built, there was no stained glass, no organ and, of course, there were no monuments. The rectangular gallery was altered to its present shape as early as 1800. In 1864 its front was lowered, enabling the seating to be raked. The dove and serpent motif has been interpreted in various ways, but may symbolize the Holy Spirit and healing.

The fine mahogany pulpit and communion rail are original. The pulpit was at first a three-decker, for preacher, reader and precentor. On one occasion Charles Wesley's impassioned preaching swept the pulpit hymn book onto the head of Thomas Coke in the reading desk below and Coke waited with open arms to catch the Bible that followed it! In 1864 the pulpit was lowered by five feet and in 1891 the ground-floor pews, with their slide-out extensions, were installed.

For many years a Methodist version of the Prayer Book service was the normal form of Sunday morning worship. Wesley employed younger clergymen as his 'curates' here and it was not until 1819 that the Methodist preachers stationed in the London Circuit were allowed to read the prayers at the Chapel.

The original pillars supporting the gallery were ships' masts from the naval dockyard at Deptford, a gift to Wesley from George III. Some of them can be seen in the vestibule, encased in plaster. They were replaced in 1891 by the present pillars of French jasper, the gift of various Methodist Churches overseas.

The location of the sanctuary behind a central pulpit was common in the parish churches of the 18th century, and until the Oxford Movement brought sweeping changes. This arrangement has survived here, supplemented since 1978 by a new communion area in front of the pulpit.

The beautiful Adam-style ceiling was reputed to be the widest unsupported ceiling in England at the time it was built. It was seriously damaged by fire in 1879 and the present one is a replica, using casts from the original. In 1949 some of the roof beams had to be replaced because of the ravages of death-watch beetle.

Electric lighting was installed in 1898 and the first electric organ in 1906, to be replaced by the present organ in 1938.

Having survived two fires, in 1780 and 1879, the Chapel again came under serious threat during the blitz of World War II, especially in the air raid on the City of London on 29 December 1940. But the greatest threat was from gradual decay. The site had been swampy ground, reclaimed by dumping on it earth carted from the site of St Paul's Cathedral in the 17th century. In 1891 it was found that the original piles had rotted and they were replaced with concrete. The foundations had to be further strengthened during the latest restoration.

Above: (14)
The font came from John Fletcher's parish church at Madeley in Shropshire. The carved stone within comes from the home of Nathaniel Gilbert in Antigua, where he began preaching to his slaves in 1759. This was the beginning of Methodism in the Caribbean. The broken fetters remind us of Methodism's part in the anti-slavery campaign.

Left:
The interior of the Chapel looking towards the organ and vestibule, showing the fine ceiling after the style of John Adam.

Right: (7)
This pulpit from the old Foundery is now in the Museum of Methodism located in the crypt.

The 'Cathedral of Methodism'

Over the years John Wesley's 'neat but not fine' Chapel has become the central shrine of Methodism, drawing pilgrims from all over the world. It is often called the 'mother-church' or 'cathedral of Methodism'. Here at City Road are recorded the names of many Methodist preachers, scholars, statesmen and saints who deserve to be remembered and honoured.

In the apse are memorials to the two Wesley brothers and to John Fletcher (1729–85), the Vicar of Madeley and saintliest of the early Methodists, whom Wesley hoped would succeed him as the leader of the movement. With them are Thomas Coke (1747–1814), the pioneer of Methodist work overseas, and two of the leading preachers, Joseph Benson

(1748–1821) and Adam Clarke (1760–1832). Clarke was a notable scholar, acknowledged as the outstanding orientalist of his day.

Among the stained glass windows in the Chapel are two that commemorate American bishops Francis Asbury (1745–1816) and Matthew Simpson (1811–84), who was the first General Secretary of theWorld Methodist Council, and a well-known preacher. Four of the windows on the east wall were given by other branches of British Methodism.

Many memorable services and other events have taken place here. On 4 April 1818 the inaugural meeting of the Wesleyan Missionary Society heralded a century of missionary expansion. In 1838 and again in 1938 there were special meetings to mark the anniversary of Wesley's Aldersgate Street experience. The World Methodist movement may be said to have been born here, when the first Ecumenical Methodist Conference met in the Chapel in 1881.

In 1932 the three main branches of British Methodism came together to form a single Methodist Church. The Uniting Conference opened in the Chapel on 20 September with a great service of thanksgiving, before adjourning to the Royal Albert Hall for its first session.

Quite early in its history, in 1815, the Duke of York, father of the future Queen Victoria, attended a service in the Chapel. But it was not until 1978 that a reigning British monarch came here. Her Majesty Queen Elizabeth II was present at the service to mark the re-opening of the Chapel, bringing to mind the friendly support given to John Wesley by King George III over two centuries earlier. His Royal Highness the Duke of Edinburgh read one of the lessons. Dignitaries from all the foremost British Churches and from other parts of the Methodist world were among the honoured guests.

By a long-standing tradition, the President of the Conference marks the beginning of the Methodist year by preaching here on the first Sunday in September.

Above:
Dr Thomas Coke, Wesley's assistant in his later years and the inspiration behind the earliest Methodist Missions abroad.

Far left:
William F. Moulton (1835–98), first Head of The Leys School in Cambridge and a leading biblical scholar.

Left: ⑮
A window, depicting the mantle of Elijah falling on his disciple Elisha, in memory of Francis Asbury. In 1771 he was sent to America by Wesley where he became the leader of the Methodist people in the newly independent United States.

Right: ⑤
A bust of Jabez Bunting (1779–1858), a leading Wesleyan of the early 19th century.

Wesley's House

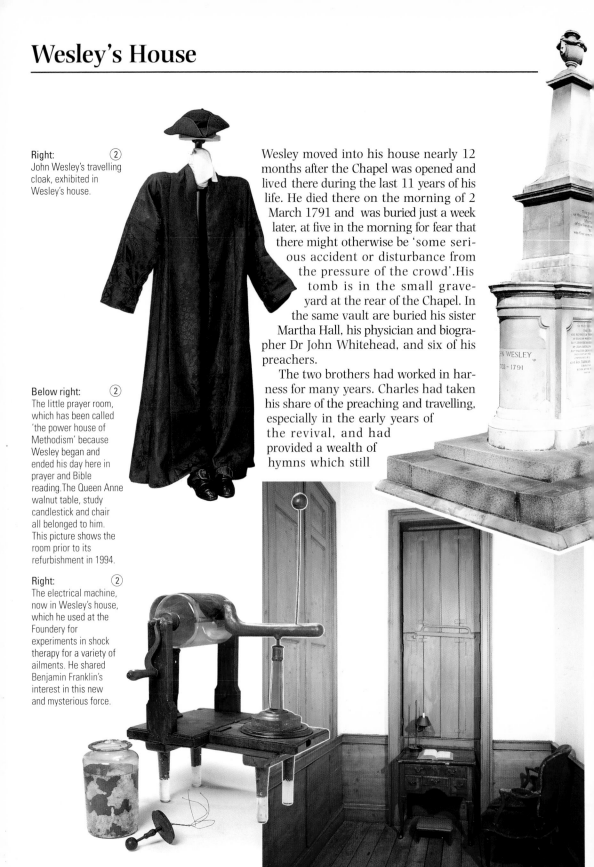

Wesley moved into his house nearly 12 months after the Chapel was opened and lived there during the last 11 years of his life. He died there on the morning of 2 March 1791 and was buried just a week later, at five in the morning for fear that there might otherwise be 'some serious accident or disturbance from the pressure of the crowd'. His tomb is in the small graveyard at the rear of the Chapel. In the same vault are buried his sister Martha Hall, his physician and biographer Dr John Whitehead, and six of his preachers.

The two brothers had worked in harness for many years. Charles had taken his share of the preaching and travelling, especially in the early years of the revival, and had provided a wealth of hymns which still

Left: ⑱
John Wesley's tomb at the rear of the Chapel.

Below: ②
John Wesley's house in the City Road. Wesley's rooms are on the first floor. The house was re-opened in 1981, after restoration by the then Prime Minister, Margaret Thatcher.

For most of the 19th century the house was the manse where the ministers of Wesley's Chapel lived, still surrounded by John Wesley's own furniture. Helen McKenny, whose diary gives us a lively picture of London life in the 1880s, lived here with her parents. Then in 1898 the house became a museum. In what was probably Wesley's sitting-room and study are still to be found his bureau, library chair, long-case clock and other furniture. Some of Wesley's books in the glass-fronted bookcase have his often forthright annotations in the margin.

enrich Christian worship throughout the world. When the time came, staunch high churchman that he was, Charles insisted on being buried in Marylebone churchyard. It is recorded that many years later a high-church Anglican expressed surprise that John Wesley was buried in unconsecrated ground and was told by the chapel keeper, 'This ground is consecrated, sir; it is consecrated by the dust of John Wesley'.

Wesley's house is a rare example of a middle class 18th-century London home that has survived the ravages of time and wartime destruction. Wesley occupied the three first-floor rooms. Opening off the small bedroom in which, according to tradition, he died, is the even smaller prayer room where he began and ended each day when in London. The rest of the house was home to the preachers of the London Circuit with their families and, probably, a manservant, maid and housekeeper. When he was in residence in the winter months, Wesley saw to it that everyone was in bed by 9 at night and up in time for morning prayers at 5 a.m.!

The Museum of Methodism

Left: ② ⑦
The teapot used by John Wesley and his preachers was specially made and given to him by Josiah Wedgwood. The original is in Wesley's house.

Right: ⑦
A chapel in pottery, one of the collection of Wesley memorabilia housed in the Museum of Methodism.

The Museum of Methodism was opened in the crypt in 1984. It sets out to trace the 18th-century origins of Methodism, but also to tell the ongoing story and present the many different facets of a movement that has become worldwide.

Here are relics of Wesley's family background – a Bible that was dug up in the rectory garden in 1832, buried under rubbish from the Epworth fire; Susanna Wesley's gloves and some of her husband's poems; a copy of John Wesley's ordination certificate, with a letter of advice from his father. A map of Savannah shows the town as the Wesleys knew it. A replica of the memorial that now stands in the John Wesley Conversion Place reminds us of the occasion when he felt his heart 'strangely warmed'. Charles Wesley is presented as preacher and hymn-writer, along with others who played their part in Wesley's own lifetime and have continued to do so in the two centuries since his death. Methodist involvement in social work, in politics and in education is represented here, as well as the ongoing life of the Church itself.

Developments occurring within Methodism after Wesley's death included such 19th-century offshoots from the parent body as the Primitive Methodists, the Bible Christians and the Wesleyan Reformers. Other sections of the museum feature the development of chapel architecture, and

Right: ⑦
The Museum of Methodism, opened in the crypt in 1984 by the President of the Methodist Conference, Revd. Dr E. Gordon Barritt.

Methodism and the arts.
One popular spin-off from the movement was a wealth of Wesley pottery – plates, medallions, jugs and loving-cups, as well as busts of Wesley himself. A selection of these is displayed.

The museum also reflects John Wesley's 'world parish'. After his two years in Georgia, Wesley never held a parish living,

but became involved step by step in an itinerant ministry, with bases in London, Bristol and Newcastle-upon-Tyne. When challenged, he claimed that he 'looked upon the whole world as his parish'. This became a reality as Methodism spread first to eastern America (just as the colonies were claiming their independence from Britain) and to the Caribbean. Dr Thomas Coke, Wesley's right-hand man in his closing years, was the inspiration and driving force behind the earliest missions, first to the West Indies, then to parts of Africa, and later to India and Ceylon. Eventually missionaries also went to the Pacific and China. Today the 'World Methodist Parish' has become a major worldwide denomination.

Left: ⑦
John Wesley sat for the young potter Enoch Wood when he made this bust early in the 1780s. It was considered to be a particularly good likeness and many copies were made, including this one on display in the museum.

The Chapel Today

In 1972 Wesley's Chapel was found to be structurally unsafe and had to be closed. Its whole future hung in the balance while British and World Methodism debated whether the high cost of saving it for posterity could be justified. Between 1972 and 1978 nearly £1 million was raised for the restoration. Contributions came from some 24 countries around the world, the bulk of them from the United States and Great Britain.

On All Saints Day 1978, exactly 200 years after John Wesley had opened his 'New Chapel', the restored building was re-opened in the presence of HM Queen Elizabeth II and the Duke of Edinburgh. Work on the rest of the premises continued. Wesley's house was re-opened in 1981. Three years later, the Museum of Methodism opened in the crypt of the Chapel. Wesley's Chapel was once more a Methodist shrine ready to welcome pilgrims from around the world.

Finally, as a keystone to this extensive programme of restoration and 'to serve the present age', came the opening of the Leysian Centre in 1992.

For over 100 years Wesley's Chapel and the Leysian Mission stood within a few hundred yards of each other on the City Road. How this state of affairs came to be is another story. Suffice it to say that each

Below:
'Conversations', where guest speakers are invited to take part in a lunchtime dialogue on spiritual issues, are an important feature of the Chapel's ministry to people who work in the City. Here His Eminence Cardinal Basil Hume, Roman Catholic Archbishop of Westminster, talks to the Minister of Wesley's Chapel, Revd. Paul Hulme.

church had its own identity and distinctive churchmanship. Wesley's Chapel had developed during the latter part of the 19th century as a centre for high church Methodism. The Leysian Mission, founded by The Leys School, Cambridge, in 1886, was a well known centre for evangelical preaching and social outreach. On Easter Day 1989 the two City Road churches came together as one at Wesley's Chapel. The proceeds of sale from the buildings of the Leysian Mission were used to refurbish the ancillary premises of the Chapel, which is now known as the Leysian Centre. More importantly, the two traditions of churchmanship have fused together and in a very complementary way have made for a lively growing church within the context of this historic site.

There are two dimensions to the ministry of Wesley's Chapel. One is its Pilgrimage Ministry, when during the course of

Above:
Members of the Wesley's Chapel youth club, pictured on a sailing holiday aboard 'Cockney Spirit'.

the year thousands of people from all over the world visit the Chapel. Many of them are wanting to retrace their spiritual roots. Others come out of curiosity and an admiration for John Wesley and the place that was the centre of his work for so many years. Then there is the contemporary mission of the church today, with a regular worshipping community of people on Sundays. Many of them come from the immediate neighbourhood, but there are always visitors from further afield. The church has a regular day-to-day programme, with activities for all age groups. It is conscious also of its ministry to those who work nearby, providing a Lunchtime Service for City workers. This often takes the form of a conversation between the Minister and some person who is prominent in public life and willing to talk about their work and their views. On Tuesdays there is a lunchtime recital. But the church is open all day and provides a haven for those who wish to escape from the busyness of the City. In the summer months its gardens are used by many people at lunchtimes, as green spaces in the City are hard to find.

One is always conscious in Wesley's Chapel that John Wesley was an Anglican clergyman who wanted to found a movement within the Anglican Church and not a separate Church. We value our ecumenical links with other churches in the neighbourhood, and particularly with St Paul's Cathedral. It is appropriate that the cathedral of World Methodism should be aware of its roots within the Anglican Communion, and especially within St Paul's Cathedral which played a significant part in the life of John Wesley.

Our vision is summed up in a line from one of Charles Wesley's hymns – 'To serve the present age'. He was a man of his time. We are called to serve the present age, aware as we always are of our history, and its creative influence from then until now. What is to be found here is a shrine and a mission. Both are required.

Above:
Church members enjoying themselves on the annual church holiday. Wesley's Chapel has a full programme of activities for all age groups.

Left: ⑨
The Mums and Toddlers group is held weekly in the Radnor Hall, part of the Wesley's Chapel building. This modern facility was opened in 1992, having been made possible by money raised from the sale of the Leysian Mission after its amalgamation with the Chapel.

Back cover: ⑦
John Wesley preaching in Ireland; from a painting by Maria Spilisbury on display in the Museum of Methodism.